# Love Conquers All.♥

DION DEREK DURAN SR.

authorHOUSE®

*AuthorHouse™*
*1663 Liberty Drive*
*Bloomington, IN 47403*
*www.authorhouse.com*
*Phone: 1 (800) 839-8640*

*Published by AuthorHouse  01/11/2018*

*ISBN: 978-1-5462-2222-4 (sc)*
*ISBN: 978-1-5462-2223-1 (e)*

*Print information available on the last page.*

*Any people depicted in stock imagery provided by Thinkstock are models, and such images are being used for illustrative purposes only. Certain stock imagery © Thinkstock.*

*This book is printed on acid-free paper.*

DEDICATED TO MY QUEEN

SONORAH P. DURAN

# CONTENTS

# ACKNOWLEGDEMENTS

I would like to thanks to our ALMIGHTY HEAVENLY FATHER, for giving me guidance for another chapter in my life of poetry, to my children, Megan, Shaquana, Kiara, Dion Jr., Johnny Jr., Shaunkeitha, Leroy, Juanita, all of you inspired me in some kind of special way, my family in N.Y.C, inspiration all my life, my special family friends, life would be empty without you. My two heartbeats, my Heavenly Mother Aida Iris Vazquez Duran Acuna, my earthly Mother Mary (Mother) Taylor, both of you gave me the guidance to make this possible, Irma B. Wright notarized my poetry, Mary Williams of Quick Print, whose artistic flair for my poetry. Save the precious best for last, My Wife, My Precious Beautiful Queen, Mrs. Sonorah Pea Duran, you have inspired and uplifted my life to a level never reached before, you encouraged me spiritually to reach deep down within myself to stir up my gifts, I Love You, I dedicate this book to you. Until my pen hits the paper again, I pray you enjoy, GOD BLESS.

# LOVE CONQUERS ALL

Raining emptiness, Raining disappointments, Raining possible thoughts of
happiness, will it ever come my way. Don't try to impress me, I seen it all, pure
gold turned to fools gold, diamonds turned too cubic zirconia, just be real.
A star came, a precious gift from the heavens above, you became the
umbrella that protected me from life's roller coaster rains, a band
aide that healed all my pain, thoughts of you kept me smiling, is
this what love is all about, don't pinch me to wake me up.
Your spiritual awareness, encouraged me to get closer to GOD, church and my
queen have become my life, prayers get answered, blessings are really true, we got
married December 27, 2015, I truly know now, LOVE CONQUERS ALL.

# 25 YEARS...AND COUNTING

25 YEARS...AND COUNTING, we were seeds, lost with no direction, with your loving caring hands, you planted us in a way, we could grow, you quenched our thirst with the blood of the lamb, you fed our hunger with spiritual knowledge, we needed more to grow, 25 YEARS...AND COUNTING.
You built a foundation around us so strong, our roots began to grow, as your rays of mercy and grace, shinned brightly on us, it gave us strength, our branches of life, grew towards the heavens above. Your patience, and guidance, gave us understanding of the word, having an open mind and never judgmental, reassured us, we had someone to talk too, that gave confidence to us all 25 YEARS...AND COUNTING.
This is not a job, just a journey of life, you were chosen for. A journey you put your heart and soul into, this was not done for recognition, your dedication has not gone unnoticed, and your reward is, watching your congregation grow closer, to our heavenly father.
This is a celebration of appreciation, Thank you, for helping us grow, 25 YEARS...AND COUNTING.

# 75 YEARS OF UNITY LOVE

Open and close all doors, roses just because, trinkets here and there, we were
bless with precious love that always gives back, even though at times we take
it for granted, love has your back no matter what time of the day it is.
When we fall precious love will pick you up and dust you off, love will finish
your sentences, dot your I's, cross your T's, so strong, your team becomes
invincible, inseparable, unstoppable, a fairytale love, everyone wants.
With the LORD continuously blessing our love, there's no mountain we
can't climb, no bill we can't pay, someone shouts, look up in the sky, who
can that truly be, can it be two birds or two planes, with my head held high
I shout proudly, it's my queen and her king floating on a cloud of love.

Lord has blessed us with 75 YEARS and counting…

# AGELESS WONDER

Time stops for no one, there are times in life, when an AGELESS WONDER walks by.
The years are high, but time has passed her by, her hips are firm, there is a sway
in her walk, no stomach to see, her hair, is like looking at the color of the evening
sunset, or watching leaves falling softly in autumn, her skin, creamy vanilla
with a tint of cocoa, soft as silk, tight as a drum, her voice sweet as can be, every
time she parts her lips, I swear she is blowing kisses, while speaking to me.
If I could turn back the hands of time, I would love for her to share her secrets,
while whispering softly in my ear, while enjoying a little glass of red wine.
It's been a long time since she came my way, Ms. J will always be tattooed in my heart.

# AM I GETTING OLD?

Father Time keeps knocking on my door, I couldn't get up, I had to roll out of bed, AM I GETTING OLD? No just a little slow about getting up to answer the door. Bend over to tie my shoes, my back screamed out "GET up right, before you break into two" AM I GETTING OLD? No it's early I'm still stiff. At work I ran up the stairs as I usually start my day, as I got to the top, I was drenched in sweat and started turning blue, AM I GETTING OLD? No just one of those mornings where nothing goes right. Was given pudding today, something I refuse to eat, but today it tasted so sweet, AM I GETTING OLD? No just hungry. Today I threw a football to kids on the block, it use to zip with finesse, today it just fluttered along, AM I GETTING OLD? No it just been too long In my driveway, day dreaming about my children and yester year, the laughing and playing, being a family we were meant to be, screams and laughter awoke me from this little dream, out the back door hollering "Paw Paw" AM I GETTING OLD? Yes I AM…Gracefully.

# APPRECIATION

APPRECIATION for the celebration we are having here today. You were anointed and chosen, while you were still in the womb, to perform task of a lifetime, to be an extended arm, from our Heavenly Father, to lead and teach his children, to guide them and keep them on the path of righteousness, to keep fighting the never ending battle with evil, to resurrect faith, never be judgmental, but always open minded, be firm, but fair, to teach righteousness, so we can have understanding and forgiveness to other's, when we are wrong. When you walk up to the pulpit, with your bible in your hand, we shall rise and show praise in the clapping of our hand's.

# BELIEVE IN HIM

On our journey's through life, we have a tendency of taking
shortcuts, detours; wrong turn's trying to get ahead.
All we have to do is have faith and BELIEVE IN HIM. Our ALMIGHTY
HEAVENLY FATHER, with his merciful caring hands, will never let us down.
We are of the flesh, at times, when the going gets rough and the
rough gets tougher, we let our faith drop a notch or two.
GOD is there, seek and you will find, pray and prayers get answered, all
you have to do is BELIEVE IN HIM...I DO...WHY CAN'T YOU.

# C.T

I stand here with tears bulging from my eyes, a headache that has me crying
deep down inside, my heart is so heavy with I miss you pain, Memories
are flooding my mind, with so many cherished moments we shared.
Tears, laughter, with so many jokes. Our families united, a forever family bond.
No more cookouts or get together's, or spades to pass the time away,
my memories will keep your spirit alive, we are sister's at heart, with
a friendship that would never part, I will hold my head high will not
say goodbye, just live my life, until I see my sister C.T again.

# CAN I PRAY FOR YOU TODAY???

I PRAY THAT GOD BLESSES YOU TO CONTINUE ON YOUR JOURNEY OF RIGHTEOUSNESS, TO CONTINUE TO HELP BLESS AND PRAY FOR OTHERS, TO CONTINUE TO HAVE FAITH, NO MATTER WHAT YOUR SITUATION IS, I PRAY YOU CONTINUE TO RECEIVE MORE AND MORE GRACE AND CONTINOUS FAVOR FROM OUR ALMIGHTY HEAVENLY FATHER, "YES" I WILL CONTINUE TO PRAY FOR YOU "EVERYDAY".

# CHECKMATE

A piece on the chess board has a Spiritual fight on his hand, a fight against evil, for spiritual peace among the land. He is the bishop; our ALMIGHTY HEAVENLY FATHER'S right hand man. Each move he makes is not by sight, but by given faith. The path Bishop takes has much evil obstruction's, which tries to detour him, from spreading the GODLY word. Castle's, Rooks, knights and Pawns from the Devil's workshop, always interfering, with trials and tribulations, the Bishop keeps preserving. Check, a message of spiritual deliverance, a pawn goes down, check, message, GODS presence will fan out the flames of destruction of fire, queen of fire goes down, Bishop delivers, "GOD IS ABLE" "ALWAYS ON TIME" check, a knight is slayed, the momentum continues, as he journeys to the ultimate goal, with his bible in his hand, he fears no man, he has the LORD'S favor, Bishop makes a move, as promised the LORD makes two, the "IMPOSSIBLE BECOMES POSSIBLE" CHECKMATE, Bishop with his palms to the heavens above, "VICTORY IS MINE" CHECKMATE, King of all evil brought down.

# CHOICES

We live and die and sometimes cry by the CHOICES we make.
Some CHOICES are well planned out; you think before you act, other CHOICES
are made in a fit of anger, rage, not worried about what the consequences will be,
until the tears of stupidity blinds you and you can't see what you should have seen.
Good, ugly, bad, from the CHOICES that can be made. CHOICES can
make you or break you, rewrite the course of history, for the good or bad.
CHOICES can improve your marriage, or destroy one, all because a
CHOICE that you made, think before you act, CHOICES you make, will
help you or even destroy you, be careful of the CHOICES you make.

# CHOSEN ONE

You were CHOSEN to be an extended arm from GOD, to feed
your flock with spiritual knowledge, to build a foundation around
your ministry, so strong, that it would forever grow.
On this spiritual journey of spreading and teaching GOD'S word,
there will be no shortcuts, no detours, many obstacles, with GOD'S
favor and grace your ministry will grow and move forward.
Your congregation needed a powerful man, with strong family values, one
who would give guidance in leading his flock, one who would listen before
he speaks, to have an open mind, to never be judgmental, with all this, it
reassured us, we have someone else to talk too and that gave confidence to
us all. You were CHOSEN for this spiritual journey of life, you gave total
dedication of your heart and soul, which has not gone unnoticed.
Your blessing, is seeing your ministry grow on a strong foundation, so the
congregation can praise and worship as one. This is a celebration of appreciation
for the CHOSEN ONE, thank you, for spiritual growth, 20years and counting.

# CRIES OF A MOTHER

Bad attitude, rolling your eyes, turning your cheek each time I tried to talk to you, you don't realize I'm your mother, I care what happens to you, I understand you grew wings and left the nest, I'm your mother, I still worry about you. You did so well to achieve all you did, but something happened, to make you disappear into your own world. I'm not being noisy, or telling you what to do, but you're my son, I'm concerned about you. Hours at a time you stare into space, each time I see you, what's going on, why can't we talk, why are the door's to the tunnel shut, please let me in. I have faith in my almighty heavenly Father, he won't let me down, if I take one brick at a time down to get inside your world, to ease your pain of suffering in silence, son I'm your MOTHER, I LOVE YOU.

# CRY FOR HELP

Toss, turn each time I lay to sleep, voices keep whispering all through the day and night.
Did drugs trying to be cool, thought voices were from the drugs, such a fool, had it all,
scholarship, great paying job, love of my life, wanted more and more, each drug never
strong enough, almost took my life, became depressed, hit rock bottom, bottom was
a bottomless pit, falling and falling reaching out for something or someone to grab.
So much hatred and anger built up inside, violent towards anyone who attempts
to help, have trust issues and everyone to blame. CRY FOR HELP.
Voices are controlling me, constantly whispering "END IT, YOU
DON't MATTER TO ANYONE ANYMORE".
No where to turn, no where to hide, I'm tired of running, someone please
help me, before the voices force me to go away, CRY FOR HELP.

# DIRTY PLAYERS

Many games to be played, with so many players who love to play.
Worldwide, players are idolized, cherished, hated, and loved;
they become heroes and legends in the games they play.
Players are cheered for their accomplishments, awarded
for their achievements, striving to be the best.
DIRTY PLAYERS, are constantly jeered, always trying to cut corners
trying to stay in the lead, doing whatever it takes, to get a win. DIRTY
PLAYERS, a name they can't hide from, a player everyone loves to hate.
Cloths line to the head, flip a player upside down, helmet to helmet, spear to
the head, a player gets stopped from inching ahead, DIRTY PLAYERS.
Medications, illegal drugs, steroids, all this trying to improve your game,
increased speed, more power, bigger size, it's fake, so when you going to
realize your ruining your credentials, your tarnishing the game, most
importantly, bringing shame to your name, DIRTY PLAYERS.

# EMPTY INSIDE

Road to recovery to be so far, with its twist and turns, cutoffs and detours, hidden roads that will take you a different way, why can't I find a simple direct way.

Life is a mystery, I can't seem to figure it out, when I believe to have it figured out, it's like an actor with many scripts, it change roles.

Drama plays a major role, like a tornado it wipes out everything, even those who think they're in control, like a stomach with no food, it leaves you lost, feeling EMPTY INSIDE.

A puzzle with a thousand pieces, the joy of fitting each piece, making a perfect picture, that life is a merry go round. Tragedy hits, turn's your world upside down, you thought life was moving on, but reality slapped you in the face, the sweet melody you once heard, was singing the same old blue song, once again leaving you feeling, EMPTY INSIDE.

# EVERY CHILD HAS A DREAM

EVERY CHILD HAS A DREAM, to be a DOCTOR, LAWYER, A sports star, with all the riches and gleam. In time, dreams will slowly fade away, just like a book placed on a high shelf, never to be looked at again. Why do dreams fade, choices we make can alter and change the course of your dreams, then life plays a role, babies spring out of thin air, diapers need to be changed, they have to be clothed and fed, bills have to be paid, headaches become more and more, the dreams you once had, vanished into thin air, now your dreams have become nightmares, reality has jumped in, from bad choices you made, temptation hung around and made you give in, your dreams went up in smoke, your bubble burst, now reality is spilled all over you, no matter how far down the wrong road you go, you can always turn around and find your way back, but is it to late, have you let your dreams go, wake up and water your roses, before reality and bad choices make them wilt away, remember EVERY CHILD ONCE HAD A DREAM.

# EXPECTATIONS

A new year has come upon us, we have EXPECTATIONS, to change,
do better, to live better, do away with the old and bring in the new.
Just about made it through the whole year, the unexpected happens
we don't live up to our EXPECTATIONS, does that make us good
or bad, does it mean we failed, and become a failure.
We the people place our EXPECTATIONS sometimes, too high, unreachable,
unattainable, when we fail, our walls come crumbling down, our world
crashes, we hide inside our shell, it will be our bubble, with no escape.
Depression sets in, don't eat, don't bathe, household not in order, jobs are lost,
there's no way to get paid, we become lost with no sense of direction, lost in a
maze with no way out, all because of failed expected EXPECTATIONS.

# FAITH

I can't write fast enough for you to read what FAITH has done for me.
FAITH got a hold of me, and gave me a new outlook on life.
FAITH swelled my pride, brighter than the twinkle, twinkle in the stars.
FAITH put wings on my feet to run away from temptation, and stay on my path to you.
FAITH anointed my voice to sing praise of worship for the honoring of my king.
FAITH gave courage to my lips to spread spiritual messages from sea to shinning sea.
FAITH gave me the will not to partake in detours, but to
have patience and understanding to ones needs.
FAITH lifted my self esteem higher than a run away kite and
just like a raven traveling faster than the speed of light.
FAITH gave me the ultimate, the spiritual strength and
courage to have FAITH and believe in ME.

# FLAMES OF FIRE

Smoke still lingering in my nose, ambers still burning forever holes in my soul, my heart is heavy and filled with misguided pain, I can't believe our vows went up in flames, at the alter it was said, for better or for worse, through thick and thin, why or who committed this sinful sin.

I lay in this bed reminiscing about the past, about what could have been, and now will never be, you gave up and left me. My eyes slowly close, I'm drifting to dreamland, your sweet fragrance is swelled up inside of me, my face is flush, a smile appears, a soft breeze is felt against my ear, your professing your love in a whisper for me to hear, your words echo throughout my head, sadness piercing my heart, wondering why you let FLAMES OF FIRE of love burn out so fast.

# GHETTO PIES

There's a warmth in the kitchen, that can't be described, pots are rattling with
kitchen knives and spoons, fruits are getting sliced and diced, while a glow
from the little oven, lets you know, inside there's a special treat, as the door
opens, the fragrance of a GHETTO PIE, has awaken my hunger pains.
What will this cost, to please my appetite??? The ground starts shaking, thunder
rolls through the air, a country giant whispers, a mere twelve dollars, will set your
hunger free, for a pie that small, it's too much of a loss for me. Why is the price
of a GHETTO PIE so high? Is it pride? Or is it a touch of GHETTO love.
Curiosity or hunger which one will guide me to that country town
called LAGHETTOCOUNT, where famous southern GHETTO
PIES, are made, where prices are sky high, because money for that town
is so hard to come by, my curiosity will take my hunger away.

# GIVEN UP

AS I look out the window to see the raindrops fall from the sky, it's like tear drops running down someone's face. I wonder why this world is such a bitter place, that's why there's a frown always on my face. The sun never seems to shine in my life; the clouds of pain and sorrow constantly hover over me raining tear drops of sadness on me. I roll the dice for a better life I seem to crap out on every try. The pain of never getting ahead takes a toll each time as I lay in bed. I twist and turn all through the night I wonder why my life is such a fright, with anger and frustration rolled up in me. My life's problems will someday cease. I look at my pistol laying beside my bed and wonder when this madness IS going to end, I think about my children that I will leave behind, even though I taught them enough to help them get by. They wouldn't understand my hurt inside. As I pull this trigger one last time. The shot goes off, my eyes get blurry as I start drifting in a hurry, I know I'm free from this world bitter race. Lord forgive me for what I done hard luck is not much fun, being so sad and alone for so long made me realize why should I go on. As my eyes close one last time, I'm trying to finish this last line so it can read, It's too late, I moved on...

# G-R-A-C-E

G-entle and caring to our needs.
R-espectful towards others, while realizing your capabilities to achieve your dreams.
C-reate successful windows for yourself, while opening doors for others.
A-ppreciate the knowledge that will be given to you, to
encourage you, on your path to righteousness.
E-ducate and share, the knowledge that you receive.
We are women with GRACE and high self esteem, never let
someone disrespect you, and try to take away your dreams.
We were blessed with dignity, inner and outer PRIDE, this has
helped us be and always be successful in our lives.
We were proud in the past, and standing tall in the present, we will
GRACE this land, successfully, for eternity. We are proud women.

# HEALING

Lord I pray this prayer reaches out and touches every lost soul, mends
every broken heart, brings happiness to those who are down and out, for
those who have constant failure, let a miracle happen for them today.
Lord place a smile on every unhappy face, repair the bridges between
family and friends, empty bellies to never be empty again, cabinets
to no longer be bare, to be filled with food, love and care.
Cures that will make all diseases disappear into thin air.
Tears that forever flow, with a sponge of loving and care, tears will be no more.
For the ones who attempted to bring harm to me, remember, no grudges,
I'm still here, nothing but HEALING with GOD'S merciful grace.

# HELP YOUR CHILDREN

Lord there are many of your children, who need a miracle, as you
hear my cry, while I pray, please, HELP YOUR CHILDREN.
With the hardships many have gone through, at times it causes them to
have doubts. Lord I plead with you, HELP YOUR CHILDREN, show
them that the impossible will be possible, show them favor, give them
grace, continue to give them guidance, HELP YOUR CHILDREN.
I won't pray for myself today, but pray for those who don't know you. For those who
don't understand you, Lord can you hear my cry, HELP YOUR CHILDREN.

# I CAN'T SAY GOODBYE

Every thought that crosses my mind, is sadder than the one before. I see
my best friend at the end, with his eyes closed, never to open again.
I'm spiritually here, with river of tears flowing, my heart screaming out, "It
didn't have to end this way", past memories have been flooding my mind,
trying to give me a peace of mind, I JUST CAN'T SAY GOODBYE.
Shaking as I type thinking about yester year, teaching me how to fix on cars,
showing me around Alexandria Louisana, raising daughters in the same family, our
bond of friendship grew as the years flew, I JUST CAN'T SAY GOODBYE.
Don't know what to do, this can't be, with my spiritual hand on his chest, I want
to feel his heartbeat against my hand, I don't understand, so proud, so full of life,
I can't believe this is so, my tears are blinding me, I don't want to let go, Leroy
please open your eyes and look at me, part your lips and speak to me, my walls
are crumbling around me, my heart so full of pain, my cries are unheard, they cry
out with no sound, I already miss you my spiritual brother, I love you even more
my best friend, I JUST CAN'T SAY GOODBYE, deep within the crevices of
my soul, a smile comes from within, a voice whispers…until I see you again.

# I JUST DON'T UNDERSTAND

A GOD fearing wife, a great job, all your desires and needs met, did you
take time to thank GOD for your blessing that you were bless with. You
lied, cheated, stole, physically and verbally abusive towards your mate,
blessings still come your way, I JUST DON'T UNDERSTAND.
I go to church, pay my tithes, and try to live my life right in MY
ALMIGHTY FATHER'S eyes, I JUST DON'T UNDERSTAND.
Work fulltime, part time, and a whole lot of overtime, I raised and taught
my children right. I'm not suppose to question GOD or even wonder why, he
didn't bring me this far in life for failure, I JUST DON'T UNDERSTAND,
but can I ask, where's my great job, where's my caring wife, I don't
want to be alone the rest of my life, will my blessings ever arrive.
I'm a child of GOD, he knows me better than I do, he makes the impossible possible,
but why oh my do sinners keep sinning, and blessings still come their way, I thought
I knew, but in reality, I don't have a clue. I JUST DON'T UNDERSTAND.

# I WON'T STOP PRAISING GOD

I won't stop following the journey that GOD has set for me.
I won't take for granted what GOD has done, and will continue to do, for me.
I won't stop believing, GOD is the creator of this world.
I won't stop believing that GOD will fill my heart with joy, fill my
mind with spiritual knowledge and my soul with everlasting love.
I won't stop believing that no situations, no miracles, no things
are impossible. When you have trust and faith in him.
I won't stop shouting and praising his name.

# I'M BLESSED, BUT I'M NOT SATISFIED

On our journeys and walks through life we sometimes receive unusual blessings, we don't understand, we should not question the blessings we receive, I'M BLESSED, BUT I'M NOT SATISFIED, does that make me ungrateful, unappreciated, or just plain selfish.

Can I be blessed, but feel I can do better, not being greedy, just want to better improve myself, we should be thankful for waking up each morning to see a day, we never saw before, thankful for having our name in the book of the lamb, we didn't deserve it, Jesus gave it to us.

Failure is not an option, anymore, once your in it, your in it, there is a new chapter in life, walk in it, breath in it, accept it, grace it, when you have faith, you have power, don't wait till the battle is over, be thankful and praise now. I'M BLESSED, BUT I'M NOT SATISFIED.

# I'M NEVER RIGHT, YOU'RE NEVER WRONG

I'M NEVER RIGHT, YOU'RE NEVER WRONG, a record that keeps playing all day long, scratch after scratch, it still playing, the same old song, over and over, I hear the same whining tune, I'M NEVER RIGHT, YOU'RE NEVER WRONG, can that record be changed, so I can hear a different tune.
Go to bed with that beat drumming inside my head, through out the night, it whispers to me, while I sleep, up in the morning at the crack of dawn, I hear the rooster crow her favorite song, I'M NEVER RIGHT, YOU'RE NEVER WRONG, is this what I get for saying I do? Can my wrong ever be right? Can her right ever be wrong? These two phrases just don't sound right, married to a woman who sings and screams, I'M NEVER RIGHT, she truly believes, SHE IS NEVER WRONG, how long will this marriage hold on?

# IRON CHAIR

Curves and detours brought havoc in my young life; I was a star in everything I did, an 18 wheeler created me a new show, a show with a new beginning and a permanent end.

Screams of the fans are no longer heard, appreciation and perks

Are no longer at my door, people who I thought were my friends, look and walk the other way, all I have left is roots growing in this IRON CHAIR.

Everywhere I go, curiosity wants to know, who what and where. Use to get pats on my back, now all I get are stares, conversation use to be everywhere I go, now it's silence each time I enter a room.

I'm handicap, I feel useless, this is not the life I intended to live, and everyone tells me I should be grateful to be alive, but in reality, I would have been better off dead, instead of living a life, growing roots in this IRON CHAIR.

# IS THIS IT

It's hard to say good bye without fears of tears flowing through my
eyes, my heart is light, but it's still full of pain, for my journey has
ended here, somewhere else, another journey will begin.
I look up towards the sky, clouds passing, just like the years that have passed me
by. Memories start flooding my mind, rain of tears start dripping off my cheeks.
Many friends have stayed, more and more have moved to the heavens
above, IS THIS IT, has the ball stop bouncing, did the spinning top stop
spinning, I hear voices, my children screaming in disbelief, they don't want
to believe that it's time for their father to move on, IS THIS IT.
Will Spider man's senses ever stop tingling, children are all grown, will Billy
Baton from Shazaam ever get old, children have moved out and living on
their own, will Underdog ever marry Ms. Polly, grandkids are now walking,
talking and bouncing around, will David Banner ever be cured from being
the Hulk, will the energizer bunny rabbit ever stop going on and on.
Looking down the road, I see a road with no ending, where ever it
stops I just don't know, where ever I stop to lay my head, will become
my new home, IS THIS IT, only time will ever know.

# J & J DOUGH

A rough job, labor job, is there nothing else to do, let's get paid at J & J DOUGH.
Knead it, roll it, just to make the dough stretch thin,
don't wear any jewelry, it might fall in.
White mask covers facial hair, white smocks cover neck to the
ground, could this be a new way to represent KKK (smile).
Helmets are white, some green, blue, gray, yellow and red, could this be some
form of discrimination or just segregation, we really need to know.
You want to get paid, J & J DOUGH must roll on, carmel, apple, pineapple, full of
sugar and spice, slow your roll, and your not at a gas station trying to fill up on dough.
Hot pockets, meatballs, philly steak, pepperoni and cheese. Bills have to be paid,
until a better job comes along, so keep working and filling up, at J & J Dough.

# LEADING WITH STRENGTH

Life is a puzzle with missing pieces, a maze with many dead ends, people have a tendency of giving up and getting lost in the crevices of life. Then a blessing arrives, a Pastor and his wife, like herdsmen, they tend to their flock, as each year that goes by, a missing piece is added to the puzzle. Spiritual knowledge is fed, the flock starts to grow, the more their taught the more they want to know, a soul and mind are a terrible set to waste.
A teacher steps out in FAITH, teaches with inspiration, gives guidance, nurtures, comes prepared with a spiritual lessons for each day.
Pastor LEADING WITH STRENGTH, building a spiritual foundation with love, faith and grace, so strong, that his flock can worship and praise as one.
Pieces of the puzzle are starting to fit right in, Pastor vision can be seen, it sure looks good, but Pastor wants it to be GREAT!!!!

# LET IT RAIN

Heavenly Father LET IT RAIN grace throughout the land.
LET IT RAIN continuous favor, for your children.
LET IT RAIN guidance for the one's lost with no sense of direction.
LET IT RAIN salvation for the souls who don't know you, and
for those who know you but don't understand you.
LET IT RAIN peace for the world overwhelmed in war.
LETIT RAIN, LET IT RAIN, LET IT RAIN continuous blessings on all.

# LIFE'S REVOLVING DOOR

Good old days of raising children are no more, we had parents
on every corner, every store, every school, every classroom, we
gave respect, we had respect, good old days are no more.
Parents of today are to busy looking for a good time,
instead of giving their children quality time.
Children are raising themselves, streets have become their parents, small
habits have become habits of crime, LIFE'S REVOLVING DOOR starts
turning, in and out, in and out, for some, jail becomes their home.
Growing up with no stability, taught no responsibility, no foundation at home.
Stealing, doing and selling drugs, for some, is a shortcut to a
easier way, in time your freedom will be taken away.
The weak become prey, the strong have fun with "others" and LIFE'S
REVOLVING DOOR keeps turning. Time has come for the cycle to end, I miss
the good old days where we was taught and shown by many, a better way.

# LINDA

On our journeys through life, we come in contact with many people, ones who give
you a smile, ones who will take it away, ones who you wish would just stay away.
Eleven years ago my life took a turn, a smile was brought to me, that lit up my
world, it brought me sister friendship, communication, caring with so much love.
In life you receive gifts of many sizes and shapes, gifts that are monetary,
gifts that are materialistic, sometimes a simple handshake and a pat
on the back, to me the greatest gift of all, a gift from the heart.
Happy Birthday LINDA, a gift of words from my heart, I will
never forget the day your smile was brought my way.
LOVE ALWAYS
DEBRA WILLIAMS

# LIVING TESTIMONY

Walking through the door, goose bumps up and down my spine, heavy
load of thoughts on my mind, I sit down on the pew with beads of
sweat falling off my head, wondering is this going to be the day.
I stand, shouting out my name, saying today is the day I would like to set myself
free. This is my LIVING TESTIMONY, please show me mercy, don't judge me.
I have told many lies with my forked tongue, I stole from the poor, and gave to myself,
I had sexual activities, with my friends wife's, instead of being straight as an arrow,
I took short cuts, detours just to get ahead, I had women working the streets, they
were my livestock and sold to the highest bidder, how much more needs to be said.
My heart is heavy, my soul is getting weak, I constantly commit these
sins every day of the week, and this is my LIVING TESTIMONY.
Today is the day my journey of sins comes to an end, today is the day, I
want to lay my burdens down, Lord have mercy on me, today is the day, my
Heavenly Father I pray, will show me grace, today is the day, I beg of you, to
cleanse my soul with the blood of the lamb, lead me the way, so I can be free.
Today is the day, I have come to the realization, that I have always been, and
will always be, a child of God, and this is my LIVING TESTIMONY.

# LOOK INTO MY EYES

LOOK INTO MY EYES, you can see the stories of journey's throughout my life.
Hills and mountains attempted to be climbed, but never to be finished,
failures to succeed and attempts to achieve, always come up short.
LOOK INTO MY EYES and see sadness of a love one pass, happiness
of a child born, amazement, of a child throwing their life away.
LOOK INTO MY EYES to see a man who did anything and everything to
show you spiritual true love, look again and see the hurt, disappointment when
as time went by his love was taken for granted and slowly thrown away.
LOOK INTO MY EYES as I continue looking for true love,
complete happiness, strive to be closer to GOD, to achieve, to succeed,
LOOK INTO MY EYES, their the windows to my soul.

# LORD IT'S ME

Trials and tribulations are holding me down, the walls around me are
crumbling down, a voice is heard in the wind, LORD IT'S ME.
No matter how hard I try, everything seems to be going wrong,
nothing seems to go right, like the river flowing my tears haven't
stop, faith slips, a cry is heard from within, LORD IT'S ME.
Lost in the maze of life, fallen deep in the cracks and crevices of no return, the more I
walk, the more lost I become, my lips part, father can you hear me? LORD IT'S ME.
My heart is heavy, pain is weighing me down, doing this by
myself, is not an option any more, I surrender, I'm in need of the
blood of the lamb, LORD IT'S ME, LORD IT'S ME.

# LUV U

Two words have brought fire and excitement to my heart, causing rivers of passion, to flow from deep within my soul, two words I have held dearly, wanting and wishing that I could reach deep down inside myself, to be able, to express myself to you. Many times I have picked up the phone, each time I dialed, got discouraged and hung up, the one time the call went through, all I got was a busy tone from you. You deserve better than this, I need to speak to you, so you can hear and feel the emotions, that I have bottled up inside of me. Too many years, too many minutes have passed me by, each time I see you, the tears of joy that I shed, cause I know in my heart, these two words must be said, and my life will never be the same. I want to take your hand, and place it against my heart, so you can feel the soft drum beat, of my thoughts. The time has come, it's either now or never, let my voice speak, so your heart can hear, the two words I no longer fear...LUV U.

# LUV

LUV comes in many ways, LUV can be shown from anyone, filled with many
surprises, embrace it, cherish it, be thankful for it's a true blessing in every way.
Never take LUV for granted, like the old saying "here today, gone
tomorrow" when it's gone it's too late to express sorrow.
LUV it while it's here, share that true everlasting feeling.
Give someone a hug today, show them you can LUV.

# MENU

Where's the MENU, so I can select a real filling course, so many to
select from, don't want to have the same meal, I had before.
Is drama a meal, I had that back in the day, is deceit and lies a combo, with
a side order of gold diggers and wanna bees, with a splash of sarcastic gravy
to wet your lips, mixed with spicy attitude, to bring out the flavor.
How about being misled, is that a real steak, is fornication and adultery for dessert,
our drinks for the night are roaring and screams, I had migraines from all that.
This is not the MENU I want to see, back in this MENU again, you got to get tough.
I want to see a MENU that has a lifetime of full course meals,
that will fill your appetite, with unconditional love.

# MISLED

You was a young throwback from my past, with one phone call, you showered
me with sunshine every day, even though you was miles away, You had my head
swelled with fantasies, I was floating on your beat, with no music left for mine.
Every word you spoke, was always just right, every action you did was never ever wrong,
you was either the greatest con artist, or a woman who was really true to her word.
If any faults were to be known, your web of weave of love, blinded me. Am I
that weak that any attention she would give and show, I would call it love, or
have I been MISLED through blind alleys, with one way in and no way out.
Will she continue to drive my love up a one way street against traffic, to be lost
and never find peace, will she send me up the river with no paddle MISLED,
too forever drift upstream with the constant heart games she plays.
What happened to that twinkle in your eye that had a sparkling glow
of a true diamond, or was I a fool to believe, and be blindly MISLED,
in reality I was your fools gold and you was my fake zirconia.

# MOVING FORWARD

Looking back, about memories that sadden me, I don't want to feel anymore
unnecessary pain, go through anymore unnecessary drama, cry anymore unnecessary
tears; the time has come to let those burdens go, to be MOVING FORWARD.
Bad decisions I have made in the past, with GOD'S guidance, my mistakes
will be at a minimal. I have become stronger, wiser, and my common sense has
gone sky high, from letting my burdens go, finally MOVING FORWARD.
I know firmly now, through GOD all things are possible that were thought to
be impossible, I clearly see what GOD has done and will continue to do for me,
the road to righteousness may be difficult at times, but with GOD'S favor and
grace, he will guide me, so I can continue to be MOVING FORWARD.

# MY OWN JAIL

Looking through the window, in the still of the night, all I see is darkness, this
petrifies me. No light for me to see, no door to go through, where am I.
Window that won't open or close, I pound and pound, it
won't budge, where am I, MY OWN JAIL.

There is a heaviness in the air, depression, for all the short comings and failures in
my life, loneliness, for everyone who I thought would be there foe me, in my time
of need turned their back on me, jealousy of myself, I didn't have the will power to
live up what was expected of me. Now I'm spending time, in MY OWN JAIL.

Living in MY OWN JAIL, where the walls are closing in, surrounded
by anguish and despair, because I don't have the guts to fight to get
myself out of here. Dealt a hand with five different stages of my life;
I couldn't figure it out, gave up my life, threw in my hand.

Where is the spirit, the aggressive lion that use to be inside of me, did I run faith
away or did it get tired of me, will I open my eyes and realize my answer will
always be right there, or will I always and forever live, in MY OWN JAIL.

# MY STORY, MY CONVERSION

Growing up MOM told us to attend church, we didn't go willingly, we had
to go, when your forced to go, you turn a deaf ear, have a blind eye, you
don't understand because you don't pay attention, if you was bold enough
to fuss about going, your colors were red stripes with black and blue.
I knew church, but I didn't understand, I didn't understand about what a spiritual
commitment was, or being a faithful obedient servant to GOD, or knowing GOD
is my savoir, or salvation was a deliverance, and grace was a undeserving gift.
I was invited to a Baptist church, as the Pastor taught, I felt like I was the
only one there, and he was speaking to me one on one, the more he taught
the more I wanted to learn, as time went by another invitation, my soul
cried out, my heart opened up, my mind was like a sponge absorbing all
the teaching I could, I was hungry more hungry than I ever been.
I understood then, that LORD CHRIST and only LORD
CHRIST the one and only true GOD was my savoir.
I am not a saved sinner, I am saved from sin, this is MY STORY, MY CONVERSION.

# NEW BIRTH FAMILY MINISTRY

To belong, to be part of, to be able to proudly scream and shout, "I am a family member of NEW BIRTH FAMILY MINISTRY".

Every family member does their part to keep this family ministry growing: USHERS greet you with a smile, firm handshake, with a spiritual loving hug. Our TEACHERS spiritually feed our children's minds for growth; HEAD DEACON expands the adult's minds with spiritual knowledge during Sunday school. PRAISE TEAM LEADER and family gather around the alter for praise and intense prayer; you can feel the spirit of GOD dwelling in our home. CHOIR DIRECTOR has her angels singing uplifting spiritual melodies, excitement grows, PASTOR overseers and gives guidance to his ministry, he teaches the spiritual word, that it has truth with no admixture of error. Family bond is getting stronger, like a steel chain with no weak links, others are good, but NEW BIRTH FAMILY MINISTRY is striving to be GREAT.

# NO GOOD WALK

Played life like a game, trying to get all I could, for what little I could
give back, each time I came to the fork of the road, I chose to detour,
take shortcuts, just to continue my NO GOOD WALK.
Spilled blood covering my hands represents the lives, I have manipulated and
taken advantage of, blood that spilled over onto my feet, represents the path of
destruction, and the wrath of evil to the people I have walked on my entire life.
Blood that stained my eyes has begun to open the windows to my
soul, where my life story past by me, images I didn't care to see.
Hurt, drama, and constant pain, the path I have chosen
for so long, this journey is slowly draining me.
Will I ever stand proud and walk in a GODLY way, will this hidden pain
ever fade away, will my stained blood ever go away or just dry up to become
a permanent mark, or will I continue to walk this NO GOOD WALK.

# OLD SOUTHERN TOWN

Toss and turn all through the night, trying to get comfortable, so I can sleep right.

Closing my eyes real tight, I start dreaming about moments in my life, if I would have went further in school, would I be home where I could be free, or still stuck in this OLD SOUTHERN TOWN, where I could never be me.

If I would have took care of myself in a cautious way, instead of running the streets trying to have my way, baby wouldn't have been born causing me stay, year after year I worked hard stay above water, this OLD SOUTHERN TOWN rather drown until welfare and food stamps come around.

Club life, smoking, drinking, negativity wants to play too, that's every day simple life in this OLD SOUTHERN TOWN. Good upbringing and common sense kept me away, didn't want to start growing roots, and be stuck six feet under, in this good OLD SOUTHERN TOWN.

# PRECIOUS LOVE

Days and weeks have gone by, I keep listening for the sound of the
locks too turn and see you coming through that door, but each day
that passes it's still the same, I miss my PRECIOUS LOVE.
Pictures of our life constantly pass through my mind, always a smile
with flowing tears of heartbreak mixed with spiritual joy.
I'm trying to be strong, but at times this battle gets rough, too many
memories, not enough time, so much more we had planned to do, LORD
please help me, my chain is broken and now it's missing a link.
You had your ways, I had mine, love mixed it together, to become one. If I ever have a
chance to see happiness again, each time I close my eyes, your smile brings me joy. We
were living a family dream, has it become a nightmare? So many gains, very few losses.
Your wings were ready, but my heart wasn't ready to let
you go, I miss my PRECIOUS LOVE.

# RIDING MY BACK

When it rains it pours, trials and tribulations will give no warning, it has no name, unexpected situations are on a roll, shame is pounding at my door, and it doesn't matter if I answer or not, the devil's spirit is, RIDING MY BACK. Self-esteem has bottomed out; all I want to do is scream and shout. All the usual things that go my way, today is not that day. What have I done to deserve this, I pray and frequently visit my heavenly Fathers home, my tithes are paid, is this a test? I praise him, worship him, everything is done in his holy name, why oh why, is the devil's spirit, RIDING MY BACK.
Why is every right I take, turn out wrong, why am I crying now, will I laugh latter, my wall of faith, are crumbling around me, will I drown in my own tears, because of my fears, my life has me sinking in quick sand, there's no one to help me out, I need a sign, I need help, the devil spirit is RIDING MY BACK.

# RUNNING TO FREEDOM

Our soul is getting weary; lost with no sense of direction,
each year that passes by, hope is fading away.
Chains, ropes, forced to think, forced what to do, steps are getting
slower, our mind going in circles, no more tears to cry.
So many tragedies in our way, we can't give up, we
must keep RUNNING TO FREEDOM.
Year in year out, the cycle is still the same, will this ever change?
We learned at an early age when we keep JESUS in our soul our trials and tribulations,
our ups and downs, obstacles that were placed in our way, will become our joy and the
day has finally arrived where there is no need to be RUNNING TO FREEDOM.
Chain and ball have disappeared, in reality it's still there, equal opportunity was suppose
to be for us, in reality it's two words thrown in thin air, the struggle is still there.
Let's keep JESUS deep within our soul and continue to have our joy
as our journey continues RUNNING TO FREEDOM.

# TEARS OR FEARS

TEARS for the emptiness that constantly burdens my heart,
FEAR is for the pain that is there, but unknown.
TEARS are for the lack of common sense in right or wrong, FEAR is for
the consequences we will face one day, because of all the wrong.
TEARS are for the MOTHER'S, whose children perish from
the constant use of drugs and guns, that has swept our streets,
FEAR is the killings and drugs that will forever go on.
TEARS for our people, who carelessly believe their sharing passion, while playing
life and death. Instead their sharing needles filled with deadly diseases. FEAR is their
lack of knowledge, which is causing them to die, quicker than you can sneeze.
TEARS are for the countries, who are buried deep in poverty, FEAR is nothing
fast enough is being done, and it's spreading and taking over our land.
TEARS are for the people in this time and age, who are still judged by the color of
their skin; FEAR are for those who still don't take time to see the good that is within.
Is it TEARS or FEARS, either choice can be wrong,
TEARS come from FEAR, so make your choice.

# TEMPTATION

Weakness of my past digressions, and the flirtatious games that you play, makes
my promise to my father, so hard to keep, it has caused me to stay. You're married
and I'm single and free, with no obligations, but to my father and me.
Your beauty, your everlasting smile, the twinkle in your eye, all this, brings
lust to my heart, which keeps me fantasying, all through my day.
Your like sugar to a starving horse, a bone to a hungry dog, new eyes
for a blind man to see, all this TEMPTATION is getting the better of
me, we had too much recess in the school yard games we play.
Those extra longer holds, those sneaky pecks on the cheek, that wiggle in your
walk, every time you saunter by, all that TEMPTATION you keep showing me.
You're like bait for a hook, cheese for a trap, flower to a
bee, why oh why you keep tempting me.
The warmth in your embrace makes me weak to my knees.
I need a voice of reason to start speaking to me, because all
this TEMPTATION is getting the better of me.

# THANK YOU FOR THE BLESSINGS
# I CONTINUE TO RECEIVE

Almighty Father when I was blind, you opened my eyes to see.
When I was lost with no sense of direction, you gave
me guidance so I could continue to be free.
When I was weak, you showed favor in me, when I was down on
my luck, you gave me more and more merciful grace.
When I fell and couldn't get up while the walls in my life were
crumbling around me, you carried me through, THANK YOU
FOR THE BLESSINGS I CONTINUE TO RECEIVE.

# THANK YOU LORD

Rise and shine, time to start my special day, THANK YOU LORD, for another day. Breakfast at the table with my soul mate, my true love, THANK YOU LORD for continuously preparing our table with an abundance of your love. On our journey to your heavenly home, THANK YOU LORD, for giving us traveling grace. At the alter acknowledging my peers, THANK YOU LORD, for the spiritual knowledge, for more grace and your continuous presence, as I spread spiritual water for your seeds to grow.
We bow our heads and hold hands to become one, THANK YOU
LORD, for being our protector and providing us with all our needs.
THANK YOU LORD, for giving us strength to continue our journey, THANK
YOU LORD, through all our trials and tribulations, you continue to be our savior.
THANK YOU LORD, for being our one and only KING, THANK YOU
LORD, as I continue to grow as your humble servant in the spreading
of your spiritual word, THANK YOU LORD, for all my days.

# THROUGH THE EYES OF A CHILD

Men and Women working harder to survive. Plantations, where you
start then die, is this the only way of life? When we leave, were hunted
down, caught, locked in chains or strung up to die. Master, Master,
what is that suppose to mean, can we please say Mr. & Misses.
We hide, to learn to read and write, whips and chains are used to keep us so-
called right. Slave has become our only name. We become livestock, to be sold
to the highest bidder, why? So many questions, not enough answers. Worship
and praising has our hearts beating to a spiritual tune, worship and praise
to keep our faith, and dreams alive, self esteem must continue to rise.
Years went by, mom and dad are now gone, life hasn't changed, it's a cycle, time for
a change, change needs to come. On my knees, prayers going up, like NEW BIRTH
tree's, my blessing's coming down to bless my world. Singing and praising somewhere
near, it's ringing in my ear's, JUNETEENTH, JUNETEENTH, it's loud and clear,
JUNETEENTH, JUNETEENTH, PRAISE GOD, MOM and DAD I'M FREE,
I'M FREE, but yet, as I look around today, I think to myself, am I truly free???

# THROUGH THE YEARS

THROUGH THE YEARS I cared and watch you grow, from a boy to a man, the day you was born you turned my life around, through all the good and bad, you will always have a special place in my heart, I've always been proud to call you my son.
THROUGH THE YEARS each day that went by, it got better everyday, at times I kissed your tears away, my prayers never ceased.
THROUGH THE YEARS we shared so many memories, we have a MOTHER too SON bond that no one can break, as long as it's ok we will always be together, right here where it counts.
Now the time has come, my heart cries out it's just too hard to say goodbye, with joy my precious son, until I see you again. I LOVE YOU.

# VALENTINE LOVE

Joy screams from my heart, as I think about the many bless years we had together, what we have accomplished, the strong foundation we stated, using grace, prayer and faith, the kingdom we have built using God's tools.

This journey has not been easy, with pot holes and bumps along the way, I didn't help with my many faults that sometimes got in the way, even with that, every step I took, you were always there with me, to guide me, if I fell, you were there to help me up, point me in the right direction, reassure me with God's will, that everything would be alright.

You brought family into our lives, you showed me the true meaning of family values, and we have been blessed with many little princesses and a little prince. You have cared for my son, like you birthed him yourself. You are my true VALENTINE LOVE, celebration should not only be celebrated on this special day, it should be and will be celebrated every day of the year.

Roses are red violets are blue, they say your eyes are the windows to your soul, when I hold you in my arms, look into my eyes, you will see how much I truly love you, MY VALENTINE LOVE.

# WHAT HAVE I DONE

Toss and turning, this bed is harder than a rock, looking around;
there are fifty-nine more beds, which look like mine.

WHAT HAVE I DONE, sharing a room with so many beds, so
many dreams, so many fantasies, so many stories how they got here,
each one of them has the same ending, NOT GUILTY.

Greed and I could never get caught attitude got me here, I made more money
than the rest, greed whispered in my ear, I could never get caught attitude had me
doing wrong on the left side of the road, my little she-devil lured me into her web
of deceit, I slipped and fell and couldn't get back up, WHAT HAVE I DONE.

Hurt my family, devastated my mom, the hurt in her voice, every time I
end our calls, WHAT HAVE I DONE, I have to clean up what I messed
up, I now have this time on my hands, WHAT HAVE I DONE.

Lot of my family have given up on me, this has happened one too many times, WHAT
HAVE I DONE, I have left scars in every one hearts, my daughters barely know who I
am, WHAT HAVE I DONE, forgive me "LORD, LOOK WHAT I HAVE DONE".

# WHEN CAN I GO HOME???

On this bed of iron, surrounded by three walls and iron bars,
my thoughts just wondering, where did I go wrong.
Everyday was a hard day, stealing so I could be fed, I wonder
why my life has been turned upside down. Bread, baloney and a
pack of cheese, stole from the store for a meal for me.
1,2,3 years have gone by, I'm still rotting in this cage, no one to blame,
but blame myself, when you commit the crime you must pay with time,
how much time must go by?? WHEN CAN I GO HOME???
Court date's always get pushed back, can't afford a real lawyer, you get appointed
one, all he does is show up, say a few words, then he says I'm done.
Life goes on, time keeps rolling on, but I wonder, WHEN CAN I GO HOME???

# WILL YOU WALK WITH ME

LORD as I take these swerving journeys through life, on long tiresome
roads, with heavy burdens, heavy loads, with many obstacles that
will confuse and hinder me, detours that will take me off the path of
righteousness, shortcuts that will sway me off the right lane, to attempt to
keep on the fast left lane, LORD WILL YOU WALK WITH ME.
Church taught me, to take one step, you would take two
and walk with me until the sun won't even shine.
Strong foundation because of my faith has been built around me. Deep
within my heart my faith tells me if I fail or even fall, you will always
be there to pick me up and carry me through, I am of the flesh, and
faith at times may dip, LORD WILL YOU WALK WITH ME.

# YOU'RE TOUCH

Lord I pray, YOU'RE TOUCH reaches out and lifts every heart, flows through the crevices of everyone's soul, to let them know you're forever here.

Lord I pray YOU'RE TOUCH, mend broken hearts, bring out spiritual happiness, places everlasting smiles on everyone's face. Lord I pray YOU'RE TOUCH repairs the broken bridges between feuding families and friends.

YOU'RE TOUCH has empty bellies to be filled, starvation to be no more, cabinets too no longer to be bare, YOU'RE TOUCH to have diseases to disappear, tear to be covered with love and care.

Lord I pray this world can be thankful for YOU'RE TOUCH.

# UNION PRAYER

Lord we come to you as humble as we can be, with a heart full of joy, an open mind
and listening ear, we pray you bless our journey of holy matrimony to be as one.
We pray you continue to give us guidance on the right path,
on the road of many detours, many temptations.
We pray you give us the strength for when the times get rough,
not to be judgmental towards one another, but to have patience
and a listening ear, at times less words mean more.
We pray you bless our health, our humble home and continue to
enrich our lives for the many happy years we pray to enjoy.
We pray for wisdom, spiritual growth, deeper understanding of your
word, for this learning process to be as one, because without the LORD
in our life is like having an unsharpened pencil, there is no point.
LORD BLESS OUR UNION, this is our UNION PRAYER presented to GOD.

CONGRADULATIONS
KAREN & SAM PEA JR.

# UNFORGETTABLES

AIDA IRIS VAZQUEZ DURAN ACUNA...MOM
MARGARET ROGER PEA LEVY...MOM
ALICIA VAZQUEZ...GRANDMOTHER
SAM PEA SR...DAD
RODOLFO VAZQUEZ SR...GRANDFATHER
MELVIN EUGENE PEA...BROTHER
HERIBERTO SOTOMAYOR...UNCLE
ZAIDEN SEMAJ BERRY...GRANDSON
RODOLFO VAZQUEZ...UNCLE
GLORIA JEAN WAGNER BURTON...MOM#2
JOANNE GARCIA...RICAN QUEEN COUSIN
GEORGIA PEA JONES...AUNT
HECTOR M. ELLISON...COUSIN
LEROY MURPHY...BROTHER/BEST FRIEND
CHARLIE SHERMAN...FAMILY FRIEND

LIFETIME OF MEMORIES

MEMORY OF MOM

AIDA IRIS VASQUEZ DURAN ACUNA
MAY 7, 1941 - JULY 14, 2008

MEMORY MOM / IN LAW

MARCH 6 1932

MAY 4 1982

MARGARET R. P. LEVY

MEMORY GRANDMOTHER

ALICIA VAZQUEZ
JANUARY 12, 1973

MEMORIES
FATHER

SAM PEA SR.
12/15/29-4/10/03

MEMORIES
BROTHER

MELVIN E. PEA
4/13/57-12/14/03

MEMORY UNCLE

HERIBERTO SOTOMAYOR
MAY 8, 1984

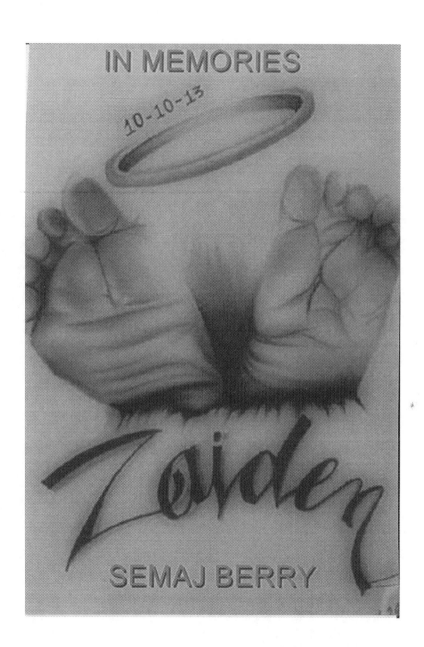

MEMORY UNCLE

RODOLFO VAZQUEZ
FEBRUARY 10, 1997

MEMORIES
MOM 2

GLORIA W. BURTON
7/18/46-9/26/14

IN MEMORY

JOANNE GARCIA
DEC 7,1961- DEC 12,2016

IN MEMORIES

GEORGIA PEA JONES
7/15/43-4/23/17

MEMORY COUSIN

HECTOR M. ELLISON
1965 - 1992

MEMORIES
BROTHER

love you

LEROY MURPHY
7/29/62-2/13/15 FLIPA

MEMORIES
SON

TERRY LYNN HAYNES
5/8/73-4/17/95

Printed in the United States
By Bookmasters